For Nancy
In appreciation of your
wonderful accomplishment
warmly — Gayl Teller

One Small Kindness

Gayl Teller

Plain View Press
P. O. 33311
Austin, TX 78764

phone: 512-441-2452
fax: 512-912-1252
www.plainviewpress.net
sbright1@austin.rr.com

Cover Art: Detail from the series *Bitoa*, 2003. Archival inkjet prints with mixed media by Diana Dopson.

Acknowledgments

My thanks to the editors of the following journals in which these poems originally appeared, some in different versions: **Crone's Nest**: "For Lillian"; **Ezine** (Hofstra University Magazine on the Internet): "Independence Day," "In the Hospital There Are Moments," "Souffle for Two," "Feelings from a Marriage," "Funneling Sun"; **Literary Review of the Performance Poets Association**: "Sustenance," "Lakeside Sinfonietta;" **Long Island Quarterly**: "A Summer Solstice Sestina"; **The Mac Guffin**: "Marriage"; **Poetry in Performance** (Annual Spring Poetry Festival, The City College, 1997): "Cat Funeral"; **Reiki Manual, Level I** (Reiki Master Teacher Dorothy Klein): "Reiki Master In Training"; **The Sow's Ear Poetry Review**: "Ulysses and Child"; **Spring, The Journal of the E. E. Cummings Society**: "One Small Kindness," "Moving Day."

A special thank you to Michele Cooper for ongoing support and editing of my chapbook **Moving Day** (Premier Poets Series, Portsmouth, RI, 2001), in which these poems originally appeared, some in different versions: "Moving Day," "Letting-Go," "His Harmonica," "The Maroon Scrabble Set," "Carpentry," "Feelings for a Marriage," "Mother and Son in a Matter of Days," "In the Hospital There Are Moments," "Sustenance," "Independence Day," "Funneling Sun"

With gratitude to the New York State Council on the Arts for supporting grants to direct the Poetry Reading Series at the Mid-Island Y, Plainview, NY.

With gratitude to **Poets and Write**rs for supporting grants for poetry seminars, Five Towns Senior Center, Woodmere, NY.

With my love and deepest gratitude for my family: my parents, Reuben and Hilda Leibowitz; my husband, Mike Teller; our son and his wife, Paul and Maxine Teller; my sister, Joyce Leibowitz Muller; and Richard Teller, Pat Teller, Stephanie Teller, Walter Muller, Sara Muller, Jennifer Muller; in loving memory: Reuben Leibowitz, Hilda Leibowitz, Lillian Teller, Hy Teller. Welcome: our granddaughter, Aviva Teller.

Every moment
fully lived
has some small kindness.

— anonymous

Contents

Ulysses and Child

This is not about the somber light
in a hospital room, the slow, steady
falling into deepest evening, nor your
calling for home again. "Okay,
let's go upstairs," you say, and make
for my hand, and for the irretrievable
threshold into your old bedroom
of salmon sheets, a paper Mediterranean
behind the bed, where your realest voyage
you ever made was rising up and
down on its silvery springs with mom,
your own bed a distant beauty—
you'll never reach that port again.
This is not about the blood clot
in your leg, the dead muscle they removed,
nor the deep bone chasm beneath the gauze,
like sails you hoisted over the guardrails,
your being tied six weeks to the bedpole,
captivated by the sight of home, the nurses
laughing sirens. "What kind of a daughter
are you! Why won't you take me home?"
nor my search for the right words again.
This is not about having to shit
lying down, being diapered by your daughter,
nor not breathing unwalled air four months,
nor, speaking intravenously, when day
assumes the whispering drip of night,
the slow-wheeling into disappearance
of capability after capability—
feeding yourself, walking on your own,
understanding the why and the where of who
you are, this your furthest journey from me.
But this is not about all that.
This is about the rush of first air
that frees the rooted trees, that scampers
the squirrels and the human spirits overhead,
after each other, up and down, and
down, and up again, on their emblazoned masts,
as I push you in the wheelchair outside,

and we pause to smell the falling blossoms
spring remembers so well that I see
my joyously journeying carriage with my baby
that first time we traveled the street
after his birth. A pure, happy moment
is never about journey's end,
but belief in horizon again, and oh
the gusty fresh air on the skin.

Moving Day

On Evergreen Avenue, in three little rooms
of a Bronx apartment, with high walls,
stippled with gold leaf in the living
room and roaches in the kitchen, where four fit
into one bedroom, and then where they moved
their adult sleep to the living room convertible,

it began with excitement. The Castro convertible
was rooted out from the rug, as dad shouldered the rooms'
furniture around to the rhythms of mom's moving
visions. He steered chairs by their wings to walls,
where they lit with new-angled sun for months of fit,
their cracked plastic covers breathing as if living,

as we sat in a novel place, facing the living
window world, watching an inverted pail convert
bugs and straw into feathery flyers that fit
their alchemy through slits in our fire escape to rooms
of sky and cloudwalls. Half-opened, the window was a wall
with voices from kitchens and showers and lots with children moving

spokes and sticks, ropes and balls. Our moving
needed no van, just dad, who quietly carried his living,
moving letters and passengers, and mom's wallpaper-
covered cornices, the fireplace that converted
a light bulb's heat to the spokes of a wheel, from room
to room, a harnessed suggestion of fire fitfully

flickering with replenished visage, sweet comfit
for the imagination on moving day. We moved
with mom's seasons, country colors and roominess
transmuting the plaster with our one painting of rustic living.
Each wall got sent to its camp and conversed
with a fresh air. My grandparents moved to stonewall

the rent they couldn't pay. My parents moved to stonewall
the rent they could pay, to stretch to outfit
their lives and their children's lives with meager, convertible
furnishings, like hand-me-downs, the urge to movement,

to free what inhabits cramped walls, a song of living,
like birds that could build in a washbucket's straw rooms.

Now I pencil the Evergreen walls, its moving
light flitting across the infitted figures of living
and loving, converted by sacred shabby furnishings of inherited rooms.

His Harmonica

"Give me a song," he'd say,
    and we'd eagerly oblige,
naming pop tunes like "Tammy,"
    "Spanish Eyes," or "Edelweiss."
Then cradling the little wood frame,
    he'd close his music-blind eyes,
to lip-read the notes as he'd slide
    his mouth along the slotted rows,
blowing and sucking his tidal reeds
    down private wind channels unseen
beneath the flashing steel casing.
    "It's Cherry Pink and Apple Blossom White"
become his protoplasmic breeze
    that freed the cha-cha in our waking feet.
"Hello again and a great howdy do,"
    the man of few words woke me
and sent me to school fed and keyed
    on his reeds, the one true thing he
could bend to his will, make malleable
    as his mustache tipping its silvery artery,
pumping, pumping, his air-stopping solo...
    "Dad, I'll give you a song," I say,
as he lies trapped inside his life
    like a turtle on its back, his arms waving
and pulling at his socks on his hands that keep
    him from pulling out his tubes
in the valley of the shadow of syncopated memory,
    "I'll give you a song," I say,
and place his fingers to feel its voice,
    as his perpetual pump is dripping his food,
his urine bag filling in bloody,
    his paralyzed eyelids are closed, his eyes,
shut-ins behind their gargantuan shade.
    Its patient silent passageways play
to him, incapable of speech, animating
    in his dark, a smile of chords striking
in him "My harmonica! My harmonica!"
    He tries to lift it up, and slowly,
like bench-pressing a great weight,

he gets it to his lips, feebly
blows, sucks, stokes up one note,
    one vibrato ember from within his being,
then drops it like a barbell— "It's cherry
    pink," I sing for him, "apple blossom"—

A Summer Solstice Sestina

Toya, the live-in, supports Dad out to June light.
Mom follows, covers him with a bedspread.
She calls to the squirrel in the oak overhead
he'd yanked as seedling from the forest, and planted in
their children's youth, she said for her grandchildren's shade.
The squirrel is at her feet. Toya gets bread.

"We're out of peanuts?" Mom says, "He won't eat bread."
Toya breaks and scatters the bread, apparently a light
blow to the well-fed squirrel that sniffs and retreats to shade.
One—two—seven sparrows take the spread.
"Where's my pigeon? ...Toya, put his leg back in."
Toya covers Dad's braced leg. Straightens his head

that's fallen. Removes his brace. In stealthy headway,
the neighbor's cat nears the moveable feast on bread.
"My ladyfriend!" Mom calls the longhair. Toya goes in
for Friskies and fills the water and feed bowls lightly,
for the cat's not theirs that rubs their legs and spreads
out on its back, rolling this way and that, in the shade

of Dad's brace. "Sun's hot!" They move him to shade.
"Toots, are you hungry? I don't know where my head
is with the Xanax! What time? Toya, spread
some whitefish paste, very thin, on his bread.
No juice! His sugar was high." Sunlight
mosaics the ground. "And Toya, bring out the urinal."

"You do it," he says. "You do it."...His urine
is a good color today. It's a light shade.
Chewing...Spitting out...His lunch is light.
He can still snore loudly. His falling head
can't find the chair. Mom tosses his leftover bread
to her regulars, the pigeons and sparrows, her spreading

backdoor network in the wild. "The Parkinson's is spreading
to his left side," she sighs. His shirt is on in-
side out. "Besides the cream cheese and bread,
what did you eat today?" Toya asks, her shades

making her fashion statement on top of her head.
Mom shrugs, on the longest day of the year, the light

of recognition in her outspread hand— "My baby's in the shade!"
As it sings, she shoots Dad's insulin and a kiss to his head.
And the little sparrow pecks the daily bread of their delight.

Stitching Tritina

By the fire-escape window, my mother's eye
had a sharp point to it, as she pierced
our heavy, velvet bedspreads, our itchy, wool mufflers

to tight-wrap our necks, our little voices muffled.
Her crewel and cross links decked our bodices, with eyelets
for hooks snug as courtyard hasps. If she pierced

our skin, dreaming, as we stood pinned in our dresses, the pierce
got a kiss with a warning—"Chew!" she'd say, muffling
her needle's long-skeined thread from her father's tired tailor eyes—

mufflers for 6 children—eyeing women—desertion's sharp pierce.

The Maroon Scrabble Set

   has strings now holding it together,
like an old family instrument.
   My sister and I played for self-esteem,

   laboring in our breathing to deliver ourselves
as best daughter. Grit caught between
   the letters of our words as we were marooned

   in competition on our beach blanket, enmeshed
in crusts from corners of dreams our
   laboring parents learned as living disappointment.

   We interlocked our do-re-mi like horns,
used root words against each other,
   unknowing then how to build on them.

   The strategy, moving in more than one way
at once, taking the advantage with words,
   never got us speaking what rattled insecurities,

   feeling in the wind nothing was good enough,
the vibrato *What happened to the other point*
   on the spelling test? And we sat quiet at dinner

   when mom hurt with migraine from harsh words
at work and the work of more archaic words
   scrabbling inside her, outside our reach.

   Playing us one against the other,
with an alphabet of her own wounds,
   her gameboard scored us, and we competed

   for love, pulled language from a dark pouch.
We got good at honing points from the rack
   of wants. By the time we were sophomoric teens,

we were calling it moral victory for any score
despiting our given hands. Across the board,
    we tiled our crosswords like elaborate sandcastles

    built to be broken, and we sat quiet at dinner.
We accused each other of having all
    the letters — BA   MA   MRS —

    and still the feeling there was no winning,
only the myriads of scrabbling scurriers
    caught by a churning tide, where our children

    were scribbling their sand notes like fragments
of music to the sea. Who knows how we change?
    Maybe in minding our children, we mind ourselves.

    Maybe as they outletter us with Ph.D,
and our parents' minds drift out
    on a sea of lost words, we find humility.

    Maybe it's the years building sand
spilling out each time we loosen
    the strings around this game the color

    of old blood scar. Maybe it's how
what tenses in our throats with words
    becomes as music all one tense, as in our

    pulsing laughter on the rocking pontoon
out on the lake, taking mom into our game,
    helping her play her hand like mothers,

    with pulsing tears over the hospital bed
where dad lay drowning in a sea of tubes,
    speechless, and where a tumor racked me

    for two months, while my sister carried
my daily highlight, our Scrabble game.
    To celebrate this calm day without calamity,

I tuck the list of vowel dumps
my sister sent like a fret beneath
    the strings of our maroon set, beaming

    my headlights toward the one I'm most tied
by scoreless inner threads, anticipating
    the pleasure achieving each other's winning smiles.

Enduring

I kneel onto his rented hospital bed,
expecting no answer, ask, "How's my favorite dad?"
as he lies trapped in his body waste.
The aide didn't show and mom's been left
to mind her soul mate's dripping tubes,
one become his mouth flowing with food
he'll never taste, the other his body drain.
I speak in lulling run-on to paint a radiance
of his grandson, and hum some songs from the wedding
my father was too frail to ever attend.
Moment to moment I can't be sure it's me
he hears or some luminous thing behind
his blind eyes he smiles to. His smile
floats on his face, a sacrament on a spectrum of loss,
defying his unwalking, uneating, unspeaking,
unreaching-the-sun-or-sea-mom's-or-his-own-feet,
unturning, unseeing being being diapered
by his daughter, his legs lifted onto my shoulders,

        his smile floats

defying a decrepit father's indignity.

Marriage

At night, in absent light, we reach for each
familiar feel, for each lone cell's soul
in tender touch, and we are all approach—
from thirty-two together years, we hold
a draw as flesh become magnetic as
the gently clasping leaves of our prayer plant,
old hurts tenacious as the mud wasp nests
on frames around our windows, we have kept
on knocking off with sticks, to find them back
again in some remoter niche, as beneath
his father's old strapping chair—he's hurrahed
for my poems' inspire, as I his aspire as "big brother,"
as face to face, we breathe into countless wee balloons
we hold unseen in our lungs, enabling each chest to rise.

Soufflé for Two

Sometimes we serve it up cold,
scraping lumps and starchy edges
like prison food, our meal like fate,
mostly what we make for each other,
the undone dishes prophetically rimmed
in the grime of our daily fare.

Sometimes we whip up a smoothie
so sweet to the tongue we can hide
the bitterest things like ancestral herbs
we sift with kitchen clouds
from cup to cup to our lips.

Sometimes it comes out too rich,
we don't dare indulge how much we want
our trembling fruit creation—
we push ourselves away—go hungry.

And sometimes we don't even know
what we've made, some hearty
fresh blend of fruit and spice,
and all the summer-honeyed countryside
wafts desire through the center of our home,
and we partake of what's taken years
to insufflate with love, our little golden dome,
yeasty with hope, salty with sorrow,
tender after all our hard work,
something hot, delicious, and satisfying.

Jealousy's Night Sestina

That *qreen-eyed monster*
that mocks the meat
it feeds upon is really lonely
inside its dark cells, with just
its Video Home System to watch.
And passion's big screen takes over,

high as the walls, playing over and over,
surround-sound keeping the monster
awake all night to keep watch
on the sleeping mate it loves to hate meet
with, paddle with, a friend's stray fingers, just
their shoulders grazing, and oh how lonely

marriage can be, more lonely
than being alone. On screen, *the Cause* over-
casts with *Promethean heat* that glance between, till just
ice will quench its belly of fury with monstrous
claws in Silent Treatment, dumbfounded self-pity so meet.
And nights there's only one channel, one tape, to watch.

The monster learns nothing from the Moor professor parsing from watch-
tower seat at the front of the class by day. Alone,
lofty light's prisoner craves more meat,
the fleshed-in flashback, the same skin-flick, over
and over till it's a tear-jerker. The monster
cries, feels unloved, calls for just-

ice through its hot breath, just-
ice as desire flares through its heart-bars, as it watches
its ticking horror show from the video museum of love. The monster
is beside itself as it tells itself its lone lie.
For lying beside the monster, at dawning, in over-
lapping breaths and limbs outreaching toward warm meeting,

at oasis of memory, is reflected trepidation, a twin-headed siamese mate
of moody doubts and desires. And so a man a woman known just
by each other learn to speak monster, delicately, forthrightly, over-

coming teeth-grinding pride, learn to cuddle each other's monster,
        unwatching
every word, baring and stroking for aboriginal flesh. Lonely
in needing more than it can give, for now, the monster

exits through the dawn just as laughter loosens watchfulness,
and seeing wings its meaty seed, making over and over
a man a woman and their lonely monsters.

Carpentry

Stuck, on a warped, old track,
our soji screens, that came with the house,
just won't budge beyond the bulge
in our living room floor, anymore,
to let in the garden's full delights.
But we love the screens, their intricate
winding scrollwork so lovely in light.
And thus we watch how the carpenter
lays on his hands to think through
the old wood, to free it
for our new history, tapping here
and there, listening with knowing fingers.
"Don't give me painkillers!"
he says. "I tell the doc I got
to know what's wrong." He casts
his air bubble adrift in his level
with some unseen projecting apparatus,
older than the wood, and our logic aside,
so that across his fingers the future slides
its gliding soji screen shadows
as he changes the hardware, shaves nine doors
to fit each kink in track that won't
lie flat, so each uniquely sized
screen slides somehow smoothly home.

So I am going to my level with breath,
and building my mental screen. I hear
the humming white noise of wholeness
in my hall of radiance, where conflict
cannot come, though ingrained insecurity
warps what's first projected as I track
my husband with his arm around another,
and her arm is around him, a sparking
jealousy synapse, and they pull apart,
the way they did, that day. Then gently,
I slide the screen to the right, the past,
and slide in the future screen from the left.

In the calm bubble of self composure,
the loveknot is my husband and I, as we
entwine in talk and touch, in resplendent woods,
where I know his smell, taste his sweat.
When I open my eyes and enter our living
room, he smiles above his book
he shuts, and there, before our open
soji screens, the whole garden
entering us, we come sliding home.

Strabismus

On a long drive through the flatlands
in Jersey and conversation, a man and a woman
are hanging the horizon with memory,
letting it hoodwink them into playing themselves
like dumb lamps into no man's land—

She says, "If you could go back in time,
what would you go back to?"

He leaps walleyed at the bait
onto a hook in a dark closet where he's hanging
a school girl's coat, so he can run
for it at the bell of mythic happiness,
and place it on her shoulders with his ungrey hair,
the weekly parties, his music class clarinet,
and the net of his parents' waiting
at the elementary gate of dismissal time.

She too folds herself into the wrinkle
in her times' mind, the junior high days
with "The Merry Mebels" bopping and doowopping
"In the Still of the Night" through her streets
and lanes looping back on themselves
with the wonder of etc., etc. —

Then she interrupts herself, unfolds
from her wrinkle to say, "Sometimes
I imagine I've been much older,
and I open my eyes and my wish has come true
for this very day, this very woman
tearing through sun and shadows beside you,
on this long road to a Meadowlands game
to root for the Pistons!" And she feels this
engine of a moment focusing both eyes,
sitting in her here, sharing pretzels with a man
turning in on themselves as time's
hardened tears melt them on their tongues
with its only true taste—a salty now.

"And I grow young as I am
back from beyond whatever's to be!"

His one hand is cradling the wheel,
the other is on her flesh taking form
from the shadowy to-be, ignited
as only now knows wish granted.

Feelings from a Marriage

Parasites! some say. Love?
A virus to Lawrence.
Yes their lives depend
on our flesh and bone.
They palpitate the heart,
slump the shoulders,
swell a vulva,
distend a belly as they feed on us.
Invisible haunters of limbic catacombs
the white coats hunt
with microslides and gestalt internets,
and in the end, the stuff of death, some say.
Yet, if parasites, it's in their interest
to keep their host alive,
for apart from us, our tissue, our touch,
they starve into abstraction.
And so they keep my fever low,
a slow, steady burning bush of neurons
they haven't consumed after all these years
waking into a shared fetal position
within one warm woolen womb,
his sun-jittery, stubbly, familiar face
dawning my morning's solace.

Moving Day

(for my son)

Movement's the only melody
                    loves you like
          no mother could
                    no mother could ever
cling inside your skin
          like movement clings
all through your bones
                    you'll know you're home
          as it moves you

Letting-Go

Six-hour drive with baggage
to see my son in D.C.,
his swank new apartment
with a walk-in closet—
"I could sleep in!" I hope
he gets the joke—and a nice girl—
maybe they'll meet at the pool.
"Wow! What a haven!"

Chatty at the restaurant, hungry
after all this time apart,
with so much between to say,
we fall into familiar debate—
"Affirmative action's racist!"
he scowls. I harbor my hurt—
"You've got no sense of our history!"

I raised him to think free—
like me—the way I saw
right through my parents' bigotries.
Too many "no's" spoil the child
with guilt, I'd always believed.

"Skill can't be judged by skin!"
he says just what I would
have said to argue against
my vision in infuriating irony.

I see many a Ben Sharpe,
the valedictorian of a Christian school,
principal-barred from delivering his speech,
then barred from his graduation ceremony—
"And they didn't even call his name
with the others because he's black!"

But he sees just one
human race— "We need to keep
government intrusion to a minimum!"

he writes his heart for the conservative
College Republican Broadside,
as I'm conjuring a closet-liberal.

Why'd you have to move
so far away inside
my riposte— "If you care so much
that partiality is wrong,
why don't you get as steamed
over color-coded, gender-loaded road-
blocks in housing and industry!"

His sudden silence answers
with what he doesn't see,
with what I do not see,
some day long years away,
my fool words knelling loose
some Muse risen in guilt,
condemning him with all my love
to have to change the world,
to have to change the world. . .
And I agonize over all the unsaid.

Mother and Son in a Matter of Days

They dance together at his best friend's wedding
that brought him back home the night before.
There's a plenitude in the waves of music
cresting song into song without a break,
one continuous, dizzying drench
in the amplitude, as they chat,
catch up—he's home so seldom now—
flare out love's heritage in footfalls.
Nearby, dad claps, shakes his hips
with their tread on the weft of sources.
She thinks he's beautiful in his tux,
she'll remember, years later in time's seam,
though it's been only days since their dance.
"Ma, I met someone," he said,
spirited with the humanly ultimate.
"Ma, I met someone." She recognized
his aloneness in himself leaving,
life's little death that enables,
as the dancefloor's weft stretches out
to take in new steps. He could
never return exactly return to this
dancefloor, looking back, to the next day
when he would meet someone, and then the fireworks
in the magnitude of July 4th at the capital.
In her searching ascent up the lakehouse stairs,
opening a door to find him, there—
on the phone, in a quiet corner,
a voice tunneling through air and water
for its receiver, held to his ear,
like a many-chambered gift from the sea.
She recognized the someone in the enclosing
stillness on his face, the mirror
she could measure herself by—Yes!
As she turns to go, he calls to her,
"Ma, come back, come say hello."

To the Diamond Setter, the Birdman of the Exchange

(for Paul and Maxine)

Tamp these edges with birdsong,
with some twittering per-chick-o-rees
of these goldfinches, these singers in flight,
you've clearly nurtured all around
your dingy, little workroom

in the Diamond Exchange's catacombs.
Temper any roughness with some delicate sense
of this nestling's down, with some of its softness
you were too gentle to touch, as you lifted
it, inside its cup of thistledown,

to show us its small, chunky magic.
Bend these prongs with some long
canary trills and some low, soft notes
as this parakeet flock's at rest.
Grind in some of these shrill,

excited screams, cheep-chitters,
chirk-coos, as you sing your wheels
to hold their hearty stone,
as if you're the campanini, the sure singer,
the younger birds train by,

so their love shimmers with spectral facets
dispersing a multihued music of plumes,
a loud and vigorous creation
of backbone and feathery shapers
and shedders, that make flight possible

when they are in balance,
and insulate from heat and cold,
a music of reduced weight
without any sacrificing in strength,
a music that finds its way in air

guided by the sun and the stars,
so lyrical even their feet know scales
as they bill and coo, and weave
and plaster, and line their precious home
with some softer materials.

House on His Back

You could stay, little boy, you could, upon this pillow lay
      your ashen hair shock,
in the grips of sleeplessness and pincers hatching all over
      your head.
You said you could stay, *only just for tonight*...Could you stay,
      just for today?
scratching just short of blood on our sofa, digging out unseen claws
      from your raw-sawed scalp.
All right, just for tonight. As we tried to dig you out, to delouse
      you from our cozy corners,
you clung to our Paul, head-to-head, just about the same size
      pants, and *this shirt is so furriest!*

Just till tomorrow, you could stay. You invited yourself in-
      to our chest of drawers, *just to see.*
*Hey, this is my gold watch, Young man! I mean I have one just
      like this—it could be mine.*
Dirty-blond head pressing into sheen-brown head, a sharp contrast
      fading nap into nap,
a delicate fretwork of tendril-boy entanglements, asleep on the
      slender threads of our bedspread.
The interweaving began there, absent-mindedly, at the wispy tips
      of dreamstrands.
You could stay? How did I whisper to Paul not to touch you?

You lived *around here, just around.* You said you'd be *going to live*
      with your *dad in the Everglades.*
You couldn't lick in the secret fast enough to hide behind what
      you called *just another cold,*
burning itself in saltseams down your face, as you read behind
      the glossy palm tree post card,
holding up the scenic side for us with pride, the other side
      of sorrow.
Your dad sent a moon shell, through the mail-order dealer, coiled like
      an inner ear around some primal message.
You listened in to that empty Florida house to be crawled into
      by a junkfood-feeding hermit.

Your mom wanted your crab out of the house. She said, *It reeked
        of him:*
And you biked your Herme hermit around in your pocket, gave him
        a landfill tour on the handlebars,
the handle of your bitten fingers, the burn of the wind across
        the moonlit metal gears gone heavy
as the night under your cranking legs, cranking the pedals like
        clockwands to kill a few more hours.
November's tree-claws reaching down from overhead for little boys
        thrashing out a darkness alone,
and no one was home yet! You screeched in on brakes, clenched to get
        a grip on something at our door.

Night dissolved all your color as the moon pulled its cold light
        over your back.
Herme was hungry! He would eat *just anything.* Could you come in
        just till someone came home?
I fed you leftover stew, while Herme scavenged at the outer rim—
        he knew his place.
And you spoke little as he, dragging his clattering shell across
        our plate,
forced his soft underside out to feed. You *can't wait to live*
        with your *dad in the Everglades.*
You said you knew *he'll be coming real soon.* How did I tell you
        I didn't want another son?

He'd grown too big to squeeze back into that house, that Herme
        of yours, and pushed out cold
for the larger moon your father sent, as we watched him drag himself
        along, across our table ledge,
with no supportive skeleton steadfastly his own—I should have known
        he'd scuttle away,
one touch too much to bear without another shell, in which he tucked
        himself.
Don't! You said you liked your hair *just over your eyes,* blue-grey
        eyes,
that held my hug with Paul, reversed in the mirror—suddenly I saw
        you seeing us.

I saw you pull back, as your Herme from an open bulb, when I almost
      hugged you.
I saw you dig your nails into the protruding eyes of your warts
      all over your hands.
You could *clean out the basement* for us. Would we let you, *please*
      just another hour,
and you could *knock off the webs around* our stencilled name hanging
      outside.
How do you just come across $50 for all these gifts? And how much
      did you have to take,
little Steve, to be worthy of our letting you take us home as
      trinkets and coins?

I turned out familiar shadows from your pockets, and punished you
      by sending you home.
You pushed away my hand that recognized its hungry gape in yours,
      for that moment,
a recognition that ran through me like water through need's thirsty
      sand that can't retain.
Could you sleep *here, or here, or in Paul's bed with Paul?* It's always
      okay with your mom.
She's out. Just for tonight. Just before you know it, dad's going
      to send for you in Florida.
Herme will have his pick of shells! Abandoned to the wilderness
      of night, you stalked our bedrooms.

Your sleep thrashed away like prey through the undercovers, as you
      pinched Paul from his dream.
Your eyes were the glares of silvered glass—hovering—just over
      our sleep.
Liar! you called. Why did Paul come into bed with us? *Send him*
      home! Paul yawned.
He won't let me sleep. And something unfinished threatened, pounding
      its urge to grow inside my skull.
Would I tell your mother what she wouldn't know? Even your sweat
      was claws.
Your feet oozed with ulcers that violated our air. We couldn't
      eat with you.

Retching, I socked your feet and sent you home to soak your ulcers
    in brine.
I told you you could keep the socks, and washed them inside-out
    for you in bleach when you returned.
And to your warts' swellings you gathered Paul's hands, and told him
    you were his *best friend,*
that Jason wouldn't play with him anymore, that Fchewy didn't like
    him, he told you so!
And he was your *best friend.* Did he *want to hold Herme?* What did I
    wrench from your scar, blood with adhesive?
You weren't my son! The knife that freed you into this world did not
    cut your blood from mine, did not sever us to be forever joined.

Why did they tell me of the blood you gashed out of little Ronnie, of
    the bruised-purple trail you left behind?
Why did I have to see you instigate against yourself, dare them
    to bike over your foot on my driveway?
You weren't my son. Why did they tell me of the candy you pulled
    from storekeepers' shelves?
Of the earrings you stole from your grandmother? Of the teacher
    admonishments you were *Psychopathogenic?*
Of my motherly duty to protect Paul who fought for your grammar books
    they basted in gasoline?
Little Steve, why did I feel compelled to tell your mother that
    you weren't my son?

What was it I apprehended with each plastic sack, so easily torn
    like thin membrane,
that you and Paul handed me to carry in your gathering of scraps
    and discards you strained together,
and filled in the empty spaces nature abhors in our basement
    with 220 lbs. for the recycling plant?
Why was the weight of another twitching life so heavy inside this
    sac of my heart?
And why did I have to see kids jam a bolt into your getaway
    chain on your bike?
They charged you—*Confess! There is no man from the Everglades
    coming for you.*

They stabbed you with the matchbox car you stole, and made you
　　　choke, inhaling your blood.
You pulled down into the grip of your sweatshirt. Your head
　　　disappeared.
They grabbed Herme from your pocket, smashed him against an altar
　　　of stone...
I couldn't say it so you'd believe it as it flowed from your eyes
　　　into the pores of my hand.
And if I somehow began when we buried Herme in his broken moonhome
　　　to drag out in words,
the hermit in me so used to the shell you somehow knew your way
　　　through...

And if I somehow began, over this grave we domed in yellowbrown
　　　leaves,
with your stake of inscribed pine in the amplitude of sorrow, you
　　　somehow knew through the years,
finding your way back to our door as a man, having driven for days
　　　in a rented car from Florida,
long after Paul had gone to college, married, moved into his own, as
　　　you into yours,
so proud to reveal you'd become tall, sturdy, working as electrician
　　　for Home Depot,
sparking our covenant unspoken over hikes, tented nights, driving lessons,
　　　reminiscing with you, son who was never my son.

Praise Lil

How subversive to praise
the mother of my husband.
Praise Lil.
To blindly sound your voice—
"to a hundred twenty five years"
from the still , sandy lips
of a new-turned grave.
Praise Lil.
How unjust to promote
the chaos of misplaced love.
Praise Lil.
How unfair, how cruel,
how revolutionary just
to admit it out loud,
you were more mother to me than my own.
Praise Lil.

For Lillian

Because she loved beautiful things—
life's wish to recur in the palindrome
of amber beads on a string from her mother
I wear now with her soft-clasp earrings—
we sauntered through death's exquisite necklace
along the shoreline wreathed with the living
seaweeds and shelled secrets we shared,
each bending for a delicate beauty to show
the other, what pearly shadings, what
haunting, yearning voices to press
to our inner ears, to love. Laughing
at the many-chambered anecdotes of my son,
her grandson, that sea urchin revealing
the many-chambered anecdotes of her son,
my husband. At first timidly sandpiping
and rapidly retreating from our crashing currents,
then venturing further, two women, arm in arm,
we were knee-deep in tidelore, scooping
from the bottom, stuffing our pockets past reason
as we spoke, leaving how to string all these
little shelters for the art of later
recollection— "That's a second! Toss it!"
she'd say, her eye for beauty
honed from long, lonely strolls
along the Floridian sands, where
her husband, a lifetime away upstairs
in his papers and alcoves of anger, insisted
they move in his retirement. "A keeper!"
I see her skirted suit ballooning
in air, her back humped with life,
and how bright the wind and spume became
in the continually coiling light as we turned
our talk this way and that, taking
armfuls of these senseless beauties upstairs,
where the refrigerator that was never big enough
was magnetically metamorphosed to an art gallery
of our faces and the journeys she could wander
when we flew back to New York,
our luggage more full than when we'd arrived

from her stashing brownies and the gifts she shelled
out her whole allowance dole upon,
with her private womanly advice—
"Never get caught like me without
your own account!"— and her week's "firsts"
in cowries, sundials, limpets, lucines,
olives, oysters, welks, turkey wings.
She lamented I didn't wear jewelry
and said someday I'd change my mind.
Her light out, the art gallery is closed,
so I'm stringing treasures from her shoreline
because she loved beautiful things.

Rings of Uncle Phil

Through the old, settled trees around my sister's lakehouse,
Uncle Phil came hobbling to us on a wobbly walker,
through years of estrangement and many strange rings—
two of gold for Fanny and Binnie, the wives he'd outlived,

two deep and dark around his eyes for Elayne,
the daughter he'd outlived, rings begun way back
when keeping vigil through long, cancer-ward nights,
ninety seven annuals in all, each a yearbook of rain

and heading into the sun. For us, it was too late
to give him a ring on the phone. Nearly stone deaf,
he lived alone in a room in an assisted living facility.
Today on an outing, Alan, his son, was placing

Phil's walker, relocating his self in the family circle.
"These are your nieces." "What? It's no good,"
Phil said. "The hearing aid isn't working."
Alan praised his dressing himself—white shirt, purple

suspenders. "Wow! A yuppie!" I said. "What? We related?"
I reached for him through paper—"Hi, Uncle Phil,
I'm your brother Ruby's daughter Gayl" I wrote.
And something shook loose through his bent-over frame,

rose with his assertive finger, and took off with elation
like an outlaw memory— "You're the one!" he said.
"Aunt Fanny used to talk to me about you!"
"'That Gayl,' she'd say, 'she always has something to say!'"

About to feel flattered, I fell off my high hosannas
and into his arms with laughter when he added
"'That Gayl interrupts all the time!' she'd say."
The ghost behind his playful force and forceful hug

was the father I used to know, now diapers and bones.
Ten years the older, Phil seemed the younger brother,
fate's inglory fast-making strange others of them both.
Neither was told their sister Frances had died last month.

42

"You look great!" I printed large. "You think that I
look great? You should have known me when
I looked greater!" His levity was running rings
around the Uncle Phil I thought I knew— "The guy

never lifts his head from the circle of his plate
to ask how you are! The guy wouldn't put
a coin in our plate so dad couldn't start a business,
so I have no use for him!" mom used to say.

Dad's whole family like a procession of paper dolls
cut from the same lonesome and self-absorbed sheet
in mom's imagination and given to us as girls to play
at rejection with. I high-treasoned against my girlhood

when Phil asked me for my story — I let him interrupt
— "You know, I am having a better time today
than the President with his blue dress and stain!"
I forgot the years I never knew him, let him corrupt

my indifference to him with his tales of dad and Barney,
the other brother they'd outlived— "once a champ
of the boxing ring"—"I never knew that!"—ripples
interrupting each other's mirrors reflecting ourselves back

to each other sitting around Lake Hopatcong,
each at some point in our lives, as on the perimeter
of what Native Americans term the great Medicine Wheel,
the great Mirror universe, each secretly hoping

to lift ourselves from numbing, cramped positions,
to shift our seats and heal our imaginations.
"Tell us about Grandma Jenny and Grandpa Louie.
Was she really a tyrant?" He went around our questions

in collaboration with raw material all his own.
The broken-loose arm of his walker became punctuation
as he tinkered with it and time, pointing till we
got the toolkit and collaborated with his tone—

"Uncle Phil, you rascal, after two wives
and at ninety seven, you still appreciate a good screw!"
It was evening, but before it was too late to see,
arm-in-arm with Uncle Phil in affection's silence,

we escorted him over the rocks and ensnaring undergrowth
of family lakehouse, helped him as if he were our father
with a hand on his head to ease him into his car seat.
"What, do you work for the police!" he clowned.

"Tomorrow I'm going to give a big lecture on how far
two women will go to get a guest out of the house!"
When I squeezed in beside him, my head on his shoulder,
I heard his ringing hearing aid behind his ear.

The Bigger Family

Around our Seder table, our growing family gathers,
our son and his fiancée, her parents and my mother,
our sisters, brothers, nieces, and closest friends,
their daughters and fiancés. This occasion of our chanting
the Jewish exodus from slavery intersects in us
Japanese, black, Catholic, white, Italian, Russian, Jew,
and atheist, that's me, into our deliverance feast.

At each angled seat around the silvered ceremonial plate,
each brings a private cast of reflections,
a private pulling from the dish of salt water tears,
an inner lighting from the sparkling wine goblets.
As each reads a passage aloud from the Passover Haggadah
to remember one story of oppression and escape,
to leaven consciousness with unleavened bread and solemn song,

I cannot help but hear the fabric of our many colored
Passover cloth stretching across our totemic table
as one voice, threading through the daily Haggadah news,
each through each, on the radio, in the newspaper,
in **A Separate Peace** I've been teaching at school,
a silently seizing, spectral-line echo, all through
our ritual into long afterwords that won't shut off—

THE FIRST CUP: My mother, the eldest present, reads.
And it was morning and it was evening. Blessed
art Thou, Eternal our God, who chose us from all peoples
and exalted us among all nations to make us holy.

> "Going back over centuries, at the dividing line
> between the Ottoman and Austrian empires, between
> Islam and Christianity, between Serbian and Albanian...
> the Serbs, they are killing just for the pleasure,
> the pleasure of seeing Albanian blood," responds
> Antoinne Pierce, one of the French doctors.

Blessed art Thou, Eternal our God, our Ruler,
she continues, *who makes a distinction between*
the holy and the plain, between light
and darkness, between Israel and other nations.

"This is holy Serbian land," Ljubisa Lazic,
a jovial telephone inspector, proclaims. "Our churches
and our graves are like a stop sign to us."
"Imagine you have a city full of life and lights,"
resounds Isuf Hajrizi, Albanian newspaper editor.
"Then picture that everything goes dark
with smoke and explosions and flames." "It's a landscape
horrific in the increasingly familiar way
frail human bodies are ripped apart," a newsghost says.

Wash Your hands but do not say the blessing.

"The Greeks and Macedonian Slavs despise each other.
As Orthodox Christians, they equally despise
the Muslim Kosovars. Few in the region can be
expected to feel sympathy for Islamic refugees."
"We will have bombed the village in order to save it.
We will have created a war in the name of ending one."

"How many more pages till we eat?" asks Lynne.
Trapped by our seats, we pass around the washcloth.
The master of the house breaks the middle matzah.
He lifts the uncovered matzah for all to see.

"Food shortages for Kosovo refugees are growing.
In Macedonia, aid workers threw bread into a crowd."

Mike reads: *This is the bread of affliction our forefathers ate.*

"Many have not had food or water for days
and stare silently haunted by the memory of being
hounded from their homes, numbed by exhaustion,
and life on the run," Antoinne Pierce answers.
"Some are injured, some have seen people killed
in front of them, a husband killed in front
of a wife, three children in front of a father."

46

Mike asks our friend Maria if she'd like to read.
Now we are slaves; next year may we be free.

       "Many refugees appear to be in severe shock...
       expelled at gun point, herded into railroad cars."
       "Many Israeli remember help given Jews
       in WWII by anti-Nazi Serbs and do not
       identify with Muslim Kosovo Liberation leaders."

"Did Mel really adopt her sons? Schwartze sons?"
my mother "tsk tsk" whispers in my ear,
poking her finger, as if admiringly, along
and under my tablecloth embroidery,
a "tsk tsk" tracery rising prophetically
in the steam-hissing air awaiting Elijah,
like the self-fulfilling ghost-whispers
that enslaved Mel and Maria's secret marriage
to fear, for years not telling his parents,
his brother, his friends, meeting most at bay
outside his home for saving the face in grace
of the woman he loved, the woman who now has taken
his parents, grown elderly, frail, into their home,
and built a rail to lift their wheelchairs
to the bedroom where Maria washes and diapers them.

My niece, half Christian, half Jew, wholly Stephanie,
the youngest present, asks the Four Questions:
Why is this night different from all other nights?

       "Why do we not intervene in East Africa,
       Sri Lanka, Kurdistan, Kashmir, Afghanistan?"
       "What is the worth of a human life?" asks a radio ghost.

"Why don't we change all the he's to she's?" Bev chimes:
Even were we all wise, all women of understanding,
it would still be our duty to tell the story—

       How much easier to be the one to ask,
       "What does Gene Forrester mean," my teaching ghost
       echoing " 'Wars were not made by generations

and their special stupidities. Wars were made
by something ignorant in the human heart'?"

We were slaves of Pharaoh in Eqypt and the Eternal,
our God, She brought us out with a strong hand.

Mel reads: *The contrary son asks, What is the meaning*
of this service to you? Saying you, he excludes
himself from the group, he denies a basic principle.

> "Surveys are finding most people thinking the conflict
> has little direct bearing on American interests."
> "Pope John Paul II, speaking during Good Friday
> rites in Rome, compares the victims to the crucified Christ."
> "In trying to understand why Gene has pushed him,
> what does Finny mean, 'It was just some kind
> of blind impulse you had in the tree there,
> you didn't know what you were doing'?"
> "In my opinion, the only correct position
> is simultaneously pro-Serbian and pro-Albanian,
> that is, pro-human," peals Yevgeny Yevtushenko.
> "Once again we have been caught unprepared
> for the biblical deluge of refugees flowing in
> at 1,500 an hour, bringing sickness and disease."
> "I don't believe in this and I won't read!
> There is no God!" my college ghost harps
> as I am the youngest at the Seder table.
> "Then what is it you believe in?" pleads
> my father's ghost. "I believe in people."
> I am called "a heathen!" and sent to my silence.

I read: *For more than once have they risen*
against us to destroy us; in every generation
they rise against us and seek our destruction.
"And in every generation we rise against them."

> "Hounded from their homes and herded by police cars
> and tanks into columns that snake through the valley"—
> "Why are you an atheist, mom?" Paul is asking me.
> "I'm going to marry a Jewish girl. Life will be easier."

And the children of Israel moaned because of servitude.
They set taskmasters over us to oppress us with their burdens,
enforced separation of husband and wife. Every
male son you shall cast into the Nile to drown.

"Why should we cram his head with holocaust, sacrifice him
just to please your father? What does he need
a Bar Mitzvah for?" I shadowbox with Mike.
"Shala Sevinaze pulls back a tatty wool carpet
in her tiny living room to show precisely where
Serbian paramilitary slit the throat of her son, Ymer."
"Vojislav Seselj, a Serb nationalist, publicly advocates
infecting Kosovo Albanians with the AIDS virus."
The 78-year-old Pope is making his torchlit way
along the stations of the cross, representing Christ's journey,
carrying his cross to the place of his execution."

And the Eternal brought us forth. I will execute judgments—
"And why did She wait so long?" asks Beverly.
"How many more pages until we eat?" asks Lynne.

"NATO MISSILES STRIKE IN BELGRADE CENTER"
"The fact that lights went out across 70% of Yugoslavia
shows NATO has its finger on the light switch now."

"Where are you going on your honeymoon?' my sister asks Paul.
"Petit St. Vincent," he says. "Like having our own island."
His pinky strokes Maxine's as her signal to read.
I will smite the first-born in the land of Egypt.
And he passed over the houses of the children of Israel.

"Twelve days of surgical bombing is never going
to turn Serbia around. Let's see what
twelve weeks of less than surgical bombing does.
Let's give war a chance!" the newsghost says.
"An eerie, otherworldly place full of blood
and blood oaths, of houses licked by flame
and others painted with Serbian slogans and symbols
to protect them from the fiery fate of Albanian properties."

49

Behold the hand of the Eternal will be against the cattle
that is in the field, against the horses, the donkeys,
the camels, the oxen, the sheep, a very grievous plague.

"NATO's military campaign will be against civilians—
before we destroy all the bridges in Belgrade and Novo Sad;
before we obliterate the power plants, water systems,
roads and telecommunication centers that serve
civilian populations, before we begin 'collateral damage.'"
"A British submarine, the Splendid, fired an 8th missile."

Spill 3 drops of wine. All assembled say: BLOOD

"Kalashnikov rifles and knives, these
are the weapons of ethnic cleansing."

FIRE

"Fleeing Kosovars Dread Dangers Of NATO Above Serbs Below"

PILLARS OF SMOKE

"The smell of human waste mixes with the smoke
from their cooking fires and the dust kicked up
by the tractors and carts on which they fled."

The Holy One, blessed be He, brought 10
plagues. Spill a drop of wine for each
of the 10 plagues. All assembled say: BLOOD
FROGS VERMIN BEASTS CATTLE DISEASE BOILS
HAIL LOCUSTS DARKNESS SLAYING OF THE FIRST BORN

"Mass grave sites, burned homes, toppled
mosque minarets, smashed shops, bullet holes
everywhere, the temperature falling, hepatitis, pneumonia,
sprawling putrid camps, sleeping under the rain."

Rocking hands with Alyssa, his fiancée, Sean
knocks over his wine goblet, the spill spreading
a many-fingered stain across the cross-stitched cloth.
"Oops! I'm only good with saki," he winks, says "sorry,"
as his mother's unwritten Haggadah ghostwrites the story
of departure from relocation camps from the Sierra Nevada
to the Mississippi River, an exodus from barbed wire fences
and humiliations of flesh and spirit, to make the long trek
back to that long sought, original home of peace.
Sean reads: *Had He brought us out from Egypt*
and not executed judgment against them—
All assembled respond: It would have been sufficient.

  "The tidal wave of human misery keeps coming
  across the border. Most walk on a path of mines."

Had He given us their property and not divided
the sea for us—It would have been sufficient.

  "Kosovo is a war for territory, for national shrines."

How much more do we have to be thankful, reads Jen,
for the manifold and unbounded blessings of the All-Present God:
That He brought us out from Egypt and executed
judgment against them, and did justice to their idols,
her whisper reverberating, "I did it. I did.
I broke up with him. And we both cried.
But I couldn't marry a Christian fundamentalist."

  "In panicked flight from Metohija, land of churches,
  land of the Serbian Church's holiest sites,
  the Serbian exodus is a smaller mirror image
  of the exodus of a million Kosovo Albanians,
  a passionate, vengeful biblical conflict over land."
  Desperate people abandoning their bomb shelters,
  come out to the destruction like a living chain
  for the salvation of the Danube bridges. Isn't that
  a classic Greek tragedy?" says Aleksandr Solzhenitsyn.

On the Seder plate, the seared lamb shank, reads Jen,
reminds us He passed over the houses of the children
of Israel in Egypt when he smote the Egyptians and spared us.

> "In Southern Kosovo, many doors and storefronts bear
> a spray-painted Christian cross with a Cyrillic 'C'
> in each quadrant—the 'S' of Roman script—
> the sign meaning the owners and occupants are Serbs,
> so when security sweeps through for Albanians,
> the Angel of Death will know which houses to spare."

"How did you like studying in Africa?" Steph asks Jen.
"I sent her to bring home a rich doctor," Jen's dad says,
"not a witch doctor." All assembled laugh.
"Okay. Okay. Can we get on with it!"
The matzah reminds us there was not time
for the dough of our ancestors thrust out of Egypt
to become leavened. They could not tarry
nor had they prepared for themselves any provisions.

> "Many of the refugees have arrived with only the clothes
> they were wearing." "Worrying about our children,
> Olgica hardly slept or ate the first week
> of bombing and lost 12 pounds. We tried
> to laugh: She's been on the cruise-missile diet."

"I'm starving. How many more pages?" asks Sara,
who last year brought in her camera crew
to televise our Seder on Channel 12 News.

> "And what does Passover mean to you?" each of us
> dodged the mike to not answer until
> Emilio grasped it in his number-tattooed hand.

Sara takes her turn: *Bitter herbs recall*
the Egyptians embitterd the lives of our forefathers.
Eat a sandwich of matzah and bitter herbs.

"As the tide of refugees has swelled the miserable crowd,
as conditions have deteriorated with alarming accounts
of brutality and suffering, as people get stranded
in border fields and go streaming across frontiers
in forced marches, crowding around relief workers,
as death, disease, rape become commonplace,
what is the worth of one human life?"

In every generation they rise against us
and seek our destruction. In every generation one
must look upon himself as if he personally
had come out from Egypt, reads Richard.

"As heavily armed Serbs force women, children,
and the elderly onto freight cars and herd them
on board, as the Serbs say, 'Come on, you've won
a free train ride in exchange for your homes';
in Kosovo, as in Cambodia, Somalia, Rwanda,
as Chinese and Sudanese Christians, Tibetan Buddhists,
and Muslim Kurds are persecuted and killed,
as ethnic cleansing, the final solution to a local
political or communal problem, an artisanal undertaking,
often the work of small groups of men wielding clubs,
knives, axes, pistols, rifles, flame throwers,
submachine guns; as the English starved a million
in Ireland; as Pol Pot killed a million Cambodians;
as Stalin starved 10 million peasants,
and 10 million died in the purges and gulags;
as 6 million Jews were slaughtered under Hitler,
and Communist China has had 72 million victims;
as Mao's Great leap forward killed 31 million,
and Rwandan Hutus killed 800,000 Tutsis in 100 days,
what is the worth of one human life?" the newsghost asks.

And He saw our oppression – this refers to crushing our lives.

"As the train pulls out and the refugees are herded out,
as they are sold to waiting merchants into slavery,
branded, flogged, raped, tortured into renouncing
their religion; as more southern Sudanese have died

from guns, bombs, starvation, than all the victims
in Bosnia, Kosovo, and Rwanda combined; as 2.6 million
face genocidal withholding of food; as 4.3 million
are driven from their homes – the largest displaced population
in the world – what is the worth of one human life?"
"Now they'll try to cut my throat any way
they want," says a Serbian man fearing revenge
from the KLA as he gestures toward houses so crumbled
it is hard to tell where one begins and the other ends.
Mr. Thaqi says his wife, who was taken by Serbian forces,
held in the police station, beaten, threatened with death,
denies the rape –" She doesn't dare tell that kind
of story. If she admitted it to him," he says,
"I would ask for a divorce – even if I had 20 children."

After the meal: Open the door for Elijah the prophet –
All rise – Pour out Thy wrath upon the nations
that know Thee not. Pour out Thy rage upon them
and let Thy fury overtake them. Pursue them
in anger and destroy them from under the heavens
of the Eternal. Close the door. All are seated.

"The Apaches fly close to the ground at more
than 150 miles an hour and can launch
up to 16 laser-guided Hellfire missiles
with stealth F-117A fighters and scores of attack planes
with rocket launchers that fire ground-to-ground missiles
to attack radar systems and antiaircraft weapons
that pose a threat to the antitank helicopters
with rocket M39's that have a range of 100 miles
and warheads that explode and disperse 950 deadly grenades
apiece over a wide area sending lethal
metal fragments that can kill soldiers and disable
or immobilize antiaircraft missiles or guns."
"Only western imperialism can now unite
the European continent and save the Balkans from chaos."
"May NATO live billions and billions of years."

Full-bellied and groggy, all assembled sing
the inscrutable *Had Gadya: Then came the Holy One,*
blessed be He, and slew the angel of death
that killed the shohet that slaughtered the ox that drank
the water that quenched the fire that burned the stick
that beat the dog that bit the cat that ate
the goat my father bought for 2 zuzim.
One little goat, one little "scape-"goat.

And beneath the table, beneath the long scape of hurts
and hates, intersecting in individual Haggadah haunts,
moving in the blood, even in denial, in disinterest,
in their new love's country-, cloth-, color-blind vision,
interlinked fingers have been quietly quickening, seeking
some new nativity, these lovers' divining rods
twisting and dipping into each other,
feeling for fluidity, Jew into Buddhist, Buddhist
into Jew, black into white, white into black,
Russian into Italian, Italian into Russian,
and in the leap between such different-seeming rituals,
and in the leap between this oppressor and that, outside and in,
a common human poetry belies the curving back
upon the self in sibilance's hissing isms of chosenness
within the colored grains within the eyes,
interlinked fingers seeking to divine that sourceful current,
to be in the first big wave of a reverse exodus
of refugees on a long, long journey home.

The Biology Lesson

Dissection day in the lab,
he would bleed light to us
under cold fluorescents,
after formaldehyded frogs
—the stench of beast.

This frog, engulfed by his knuckles,
was alive!

And we were summoned to watch
the insignificance of its pea-green flesh,
squirming,
as he stretched it out on a block of wood.

It was alive
as he plunged in a pin
through the left little leg—
its well-shaped muscles immobilized.

It was alive
as he pierced through the right
with its two little scars.

The point of the lesson—
the course of blood—
so no anesthesia. *It would
stop the heart*, he said.

One arm got free and reached
into air, waving,
pushing against his omnipotent thumb.

An inexplicable smile spread across his face
before he stabbed the pin
through that freed little hand.

The last limb was easiest—
the pin slid right in.

Pinned alive, so we might receive it,
a frog, O God, it was just a frog—
I wanted to run—
but the lesson wasn't over.

It was alive
as he sliced open the arm
that had waved,
peeled back the thin skin,
pinned it open.

A stain spread over
the block. Flowing
down the sides of the wood,
its life began
leaking away
as sand in an hourglass.

Hurry and look! he admonished
and set the scope on a beating vessel
so we might bear witness—
and there it was—his smile
again, a flickering lesson
of little head spears.

Then he worked with his blade,
cracked open its small
heaving chest, and revealed
its naked, pulsating heart—

akin to our sanctuary
whose distant throbbing he
could not hear beneath the blade
of his Caesarean delivery into death
in the stink of knowledge.

My turn, told to look in,
I thought of Hawthorne's Dr. Chillingworth,
the probing violation
of a living heart—

and wanted to run—but the lesson
wasn't over—and I looked in—
because he told me to.

It was a lesson of flesh
and tissue and tears, taking
thirty years, but it's
not over yet—to see—

To see all the delicate, fragile
layers of life that could be pierced,
punctured, peeled back, and probed,
who could count the creative ways,
with acid or rope or electric prods,
unscrambling DNA and high-tech bugs
for all the ferocity of bioterrorism,
skin scorched, bones broken, hearts exposed,
the black shadow dangling
from the tree of life.

And I have wondered down the toll
of years since my first compliance,
How else? How else?

Genome Project Update

Researchers say a gene
somewhere on chromosome 13
is linked to war. Ironically,
this very chromosome 13
was found to contain a gene
linked to primary enuresis,
bed-wetting, in children especially.
They say it was sheer serendipity
that put them on to 13's
long arm for their discovery
of not exactly the site, only
the gene's general vicinity.
And it very probably
isn't the entire story,
not the only involved gene.
They distinguish belligerency
by two patterns, like enuresis.
In primary enuresis or belligerency,
children fight or bed-pee
at least three times a week,
or act in ways that are likely
to provoke fights. Pediatricians
say this accounts for 73
percent of the cases. Reporting
how involved families were relieved
to learn the cause was genetic,
thus beyond the control of either
parent or child, researchers
say that knowing a gene
is causing the problem alleviates
how we're often made to feel
the stigma, the blame. For the discovery
shows the problem is not emotional.
As for treatment, a sensor in sheets
that sets off a bell detector
to help children with the ability
to sense night fullness will be restudied,
to see if our behavior can be rekeyed
by alerting to the links between
our anger and fear, in sweat and pee.

The Cause

Researchers now know our ultimate cause
is germs, for most woes haunting humanity,
down through the ages of cancer, palsy, diabetes,
hardened arteries and other disorders of the heart,
sclerosis, even Alzheimer's—you name it.

The cause is not in our genes, they thank God,
for genetic defects would reduce fitness to reproduce,
or parent well, and would get factored out
by time, they say. Look to the cosmos of the micro—
how billions, blink, gadzillions embed this line.

It's not in the way we eat, worry, or hate,
hallelujah! We've been absolved. Take ulcers—
the cause is not in ourselves after all.
The inner deterioration comes from without,
the devil an existentially implanted microbe.

So we can pig-out on stress without guilt,
and antibiotically bomb to health in our sleep.
Take childhood syphilis, once thought as punishment
for the father's sins, now reduced to a spirochete.
The cause is not in ourselves any more.

Even the chronic keepers of human happiness
bear the signatures of bacterial graphics,
they say. Take depression and schizophrenia,
eating disorders, even homosexual desire—
they've been around for a long, long time.

And the nearly infinite universe of micro-aliens,
these super subtle harborers in living nuance
can commandeer our human machinery for years
and keep us alive for their own Darwinian deals.
Who knows how long the incubation is!

Maybe a lifetime from some source to symptom.
Talent too may be a disease. How freeing!
Just some bizarre bacterial mutation to keep

the host happy long enough for contagion.
How many bacteria can dance on the head of a pen?

Can we write-in tyranny, bigotry, intolerance?
They've been around for a long, long time.
Maybe germs are the missing black matter
of the universe, so slick they can fit
inside an idea to spread their kind.

Keeping cultures pure, what a germ of an idea
leading to the gas chamber and guided missile.
The cause is not in ourselves any more.
Already poised pathogens are commandeering machinery
all over the world to spread their kind.

Dangling Lives

Dangling constructions
after "The Truman Show"

Entangled in the ropes of his existence
that doublecrossed him as any Christ, lying nearly
drowned at the prow of his

little boat, being watched
in his effete efforts to escape by sea
when the worst buttons were pressed:

typhonic wind, titanic
waves, thundering hurricane, and we feeling
through his true-human panic

here being something to hang
on to as we dangling in our bunched, escapee seats,
cargoed with our billeted beings;

then his prow crashing through
his worldome edge as universal skin as we
thinking Columbus, Glenn, Freud,

Martin Luther King, and his walking
on water, ascending the staircase in rainbow resplendency,
to get the shaft in the domed sky

when finding God is just
another projectionist mogul, a hi-tech, Hollywood circuitry,
with everyone in on it:

parents and teachers, friends
and preachers— "Southern Baptists declaring belief
'wife should submit to husband'";

"Argentina accusing a former leader
of ordering kidnappings of children during the 70's
and 80's 'dirty war'"—

our being all kidnapped children,
starring in our own sealed domes, seeking
the exit door with Truman,

unconscious in prime time's power,
chips off the old family sitcom screens,
Mendel a Nielsen monitor,

the Culture Cable Network's
equalizing pulse setting our photoelectric cells detecting
our slight, sleight breakouts,

desperate to get into the main clause
of this supercoiled contract, agents of our own beings,
down on all fours,

or up on our heads,
doing yoga and drugs, genomes and deep breathing,
voodoo, rosaries, and the World Wide Web.

Independence Day

Our heads tilted upward to amazement
at the colors interblossoming
like bursts of laughter across our dark night—

maybe the only thing left to distinguish us—

the fireworks' beauty quieting our fear of death
soldiers stomached in the human mud of evolution—
knowing at any given moment a war is on somewhere—

I loved the laughter I heard on that lawn
so vast it held the brightness of thousands of lives
cohabitating for thirty years now—

despite their private fires—

in their towering Co-op City Bronx apartments
where I might have grown
if not for the feared ethnicities—

the color dread—my parents made us flee to Queens—

All day like some auspicious procession
I watched with an old friend who lived here—
people overlapping their spreads—

their lively games—their a cappella dance—

their ethnic picnics—their egg-opening children—
their luminous miscellaneous joys of being outdoors—
their friendships the fireworks

blossoming across the colors of their lives—

Salem Recovery

"Accusations of witchcraft
punctuate the periodic crises"—
Clyde Mitchell among the Yao and
Victor Turner among the Ndembu

Burning through my flannel bedstakes,
my broom flying at night because
I couldn't sleep, I'd sweep, snap heads
off animal cookies, ambush the peace.

My cauldron, my body, my betrayer, turning
me in. Even the Revisionist Hypnotist
didn't get it. The witch trials were for women—
it's crystal clear now—women in menopause.

The good judges—men. "Aha!" he muttered.
"Now we're getting somewhere," and he
hanged me up on the cord of my mother.
"Let her rot!" he declaimed and entranced me.

I cried. My hands and legs went numb.
He invoked an Ear-Nose-Throat Man
for my bloated underwater sinus purgation.
No atheists in foxholes or Menopause, Salem.

Refusing to believe, my head lit up
like a jack-o'-lantern by the powerful beacon
of the Ear-Nose-Throat Disciple,
whose accusation was allergy of unknown origin,

and who proclaimed he could work wonders
with an ordeal by laser beam and anesthesia.
The Voodoo Allergist made me a pincushion,
absolved my herb diet and cat familiars,

and spelled out the Technician Shaman
for a scan by his clairvoyant CAT
with cold x-ray eyes through my migraine,
where concrete blocks of pain sat.

Healthy is invisible. Happy
materializes retrospectively. A Coalition
Government of Medicine Men must presume
concretion: so "chronic maxillaries" the condition.

They ordered antibiotics to kill
any demonic bugs lurking within,
something for sleep, cramps, and a trial
by decongestants: Vancenase, Duravent, Tysine.

A Chiropractor took my chains of pain
as spinal. My very words hurt
as I spoke, and the English Chairman questioned
my sudden drop in student ratings.

When Mike stressed there was only so much
one could take— "Give her Prozac"—
and the Allergist agreed, pain being such
a lonely place, I took one. Spat

it down the drain, and made a compact
to go the distance alone, in an immensity
of need, uncharmed by any magic.
This trial was long. As always, epiphanies

didn't come. But after sinking thousands
into our basement to pump out mold and mildew,
waterproofing, painting, blaming the Conservatives
for contaminating our water and food,

for poisoning the air, after the warning
by the Gynecologist— "You'll dry up like
an old hag in there without estrogen!"—
and after reading of menopause in Japan, my

discovery of soy—tofu or beans,
protein powder or milk—give me
each day my daily soy. I eat
soy; therefore, I am—after seeing

through Hecate, mother of all scapegoats,
how crises breed need to blame—
Forgive me—I still refuse to believe
in helping each other we're doomed to fail—

O humanity.

Acoustic Neuroma

(To Mike)

Under the summer awning sheeted with rain,
you shared my realization
I was losing my hearing in one ear,
had to weigh the worth of my words,
for each utterance vibrated with pain.
As we dined outdoors at a New England inn,
chewing setting off firecrackers in my head,
stray noises of cars, revelers, competing with your voice,
and as we wandered through our vacation week
like pilgrims in bewilderment,
you picked up my conversation's slack,
weaving comfort and story from stray strands
of the little communal woods marriage makes,
this our 35th year of learning to nestle our frailties
in each other, of learning to believe in
a kind of hearing the back of the mind.
Missing words, I could see your resonance
in the extremity of that common light
projecting us larger than ourselves.

And when I was strapped into the gimlet-eyed dark
and dye-shot for revelation,
when I went sliding down the long, lonely tunnel of who I am
magnetically drawing me as I chanted for calmness,
under a cold, atonal jackhammer to terror,
your voice was the last and first float I clung to
before the surging, swirling sentencing of being—
Tumor—Auditory Nerve—Pressing Your Brain—
Five Years Tops—Unless—I've Already Explained—
Phase One—Just Touching—Unless We're Lucky
—Stroke—Percent Meningitis—Percent Per-Vertigo
—Per—I Thought I Made That Clear?—Percent—
Balance Nerve—Per—Facial Nerve—Per-Sagging
Percent—Per-Walking Like You're Drunk—Lucky.

When I was flanked with the evidence of me,
grey pictures of my grey matter

68

in matter-of-fact fluorescent radiance,
when I denied my name, an etched negative space,
you blurred out the world to see me with tears
down your face I streamed to newfound stillness.

During the long waiting days missing the days
when health was invisible, when I was
carrying an alien life form with an agenda all its own—
"Invasion of the Body Snatchers," my free-verse neuroma,
a growing concretion of purposelessness, and the less
I could hear, the more I could hear its solipsistic hiss—
when I was waiting for the surgeon's light,
you delivered me from hearing only me
echoing down my hermit cochlear shell.
You were my designated worrier, the more you
patrolled the night's impulses, the safer I felt.

And when I shed gravity with my clothes and hair,
rode gurneys away from my body, the only temple I knew,
woke indignant at everyone's standing sideways,
when the inner springs of the world were trembling
with absolute senselessness so I shut my eyes
for whirlinglessness into timelessness,
orphaned by illness into institution's hive
with flitting, shifting, stinging workers,
droning machines dripping and buzzing all around,
wearing flyaway gowns unwrapping dignity
with vestigial wings to nowhere but the john,
and every touch was for some procedure—

When I was stapled across my abdomen
for the fat they took to fill the gap in my skull,
my head bandaged like a war victim's,
and every part of my body got invaded,
my spine punctured with a lumbar drain
guided by a long needle that shot electric
down my leg with risks of paralysis,
an endless week of hourly spinal taps,
a spigot in my back turned on and off like a tree
sapped, rooted to its gravebed—

skin-to-skin, your touch worked out
the lonely kinks in my heart.

Long nights awake, dreamless, cradling
a stuffed cat, when I left myself outside
and watched me like a movie of someone else,
you arrived each morning, your smile my focusing beam
behind the fractured images projected in my theater,
and you sat by my side, empowered my sleep into dream,
you sat by my side, empowered my sore locked jaw to eat,
you sat by my side, empowered my boredom into Scrabble play,
and we played as lovers instinctively harvest in gloom.

Not all the support group, web site, sylvan mind control,
shul, church, Reiki Master, EST waves and props,
not the words of our psychologist friend:
I won't bother you while you're going through your ordeal,
nor the *I love you too* I'd told well-meaning friends
at the last supper, the movie, the let's-not-talk-about-it
chatter, their good-bye hug a little tighter,
my leaving them standing there, their
watching me drive off in their hearse
looks in their eyes, were as merciful
as the hook of your arm, the pull of your pale face,
the clasp of our lives, the shine of your tears.

And when my horizon had no weather, no sense
of day or night, when I was bound by bars
and fevered with meningitis, packed in ice
like a fish, paralyzed with edema's expanding pain,
the hours dripping corrosively with antibiotics
burning my veins, you sat by my side,
slumped by the long days, the weeks, the months,
refusing to leave me alone to the witching hours,
no nurses around, my vein burst into vancomycin tears,
the gown soaking in my medicine,
the warning of the old, overworked nurse echoing:
Now nobody buzz me! I got a lot to do tonight!
only a well-intentioned student around with his lance
geysering four of my veins before giving up to apology,
you vowed you wouldn't let that happen again,

and you sat by my side patrolling my treatments
through unheard reruns of Lucy and Gleason.

And when I was pausing at a portal into howling space,
you were my persistent reminder all through my flesh
to deny nothingness, to want to pull tomatoes
from a fist of manure in our backyard,
to miss our furniture shaped by our presence,
to envision carrying a roast beef to my mother—
say, I'm home! from my bogus Boston seminar,
to flow into the germinating horizon of our son,
to need the knead of our cats Relish and Spicy on my belly,
to put the razor blade to the masking tape
on our windows, see how the hurricane passes,
to believe how histrionic, how overrated death is,
you were my persistent reminder all through my flesh
of the feel and the smell and the awareness
of each sweet momentousness, each rich goodness
savory on my tongue, releasing healing experience.

In the Hospital There Are Moments

When Tara, my Hindu roommate, stricken
speechless and paralyzed by stroke,
streams into tears as I lift
· her fallen gown back onto her shoulder
and she leans forward for a hug,

when I say "Good night, Roomy"
to the black woman with MS who's been
in and out of this ward since 1987
and she pulls open the curtain between us
and moonlight streams on my bed,

when the Polish woman on the gurney
on her way to surgery at 5 a.m.
grasps my hand I've wriggled my way
to the edge of my bed to offer
with a stream of wishes for luck and time,

there are moments I know my self
and the totality of the universe are no different,
moments my mind is in every cell of my body.

Terry

Friends, since we were 14—
she's let me learn about her
native self, what threads

the diverse possibilities of her
life's myriad phases—
young wife, devoted mother,

artist brushing flight,
divorcee, sales rep for
Tupperware and Fuller Brush,

paralegal secretary, rock
hunter, astronomy jamboreer,
born-again Jew,

camper—to name a few
of what I cannot name in
mother, teacher, consoler,

sister dreamer who looks back
to look ahead, in an ongoing story
of how we fuel each other's lives

and so deep heat our own,
with its ease in how it holds
worry, wrongs, weariness,

grief and pleasures in a single plot
to forgive what we need not be,
to praise our sufficiency.

No one gives this story's energy
away, it can only come back
in the tide rippling history,

and the soothing bounty in familiarity.

Reiki Master in Training

When Terry tells me she wants to be
my conduit of universal energy,
I chuckle, amused with curiosity.

She opens her Reiki Guide, and we
arrange the chairs as in Figure #3.
Learning healing, she's practicing on me.

She says she's sorry for forgetting to remember
Pachelbel's *Canon*, sounds of the sea.
We'll have to imagine our own soothing ditty,

she says, dimming the lights on my teeheeing
and turning my hands up on my knees.
She places her hands on my head, leans—

Position #1. Nothing really seems
happening. She flips pages to see
what's next, still learning, she's sorry.

I say, *I'm sure glad that my surgeon
didn't work this way,* sure Tim Conway's behind
her hands, that somehow astonish my ease

as they touch my face and she's telling me
she's going to *learn the art of healing
long-distance, like Edgar Cayce.*

Position #3. And all the while we're speaking
in shadowy light, through trust's meandering
openings for forty years to get us here.

Her hands on my shoulders—I feel heat—
an inexplicably penetrating—mind-belittling—
blossoming heat—and my arms—my legs comprehend

as in meditation—a numbing peaceful regard—
regardless of how or why—a rising heat
where spirit loves form releasing

friendship's healing—
a radiant heat between
what was and is to be.

"Gableshu"

With only minutes left, and yet
students lift their heads from a test
to say "Bless you!" to a sneezer.
Drifting at my desk, I wonder

why there is no "Bless you!" for coughs,
or coitus, flatulence, or mouthing off,
when each, like a sneeze, is a spraying out,
through which it was believed, your soul left

your body to fend on its own unholiness.
Did they think the soul left only through the nose?
Then what's the upshot of having two nostrils?
That could lead to divided souls,

lots of expelled, divided souls,
free-floating, unblessed, in the universe alone.
I hate to think some poor sneezer
or wheezer was left a soulless geezer

because I was the sole unblessing bystander,
distracted in my garden from my tie to this passerby
during rose, cold, or hay fever,
flu, spore, smog, or whatever

season for sneezing. Yet I must confess,
as a teen atheist, I took an oath of non-blessing,
seeing the quick-fix, knee-jerk comment
at a reflexive sneeze as no skin

off the blesser's nose, while the charlatan
in sheepskin blessing of good samaritan
would likely sly away at the slightest personal jeopardy,
so a cheap "Bless you!" was just hypocrisy.

Loafing at ease, I invited my sneeze
by looking up at the sun to release
a little tickle in my nose this morning
and hoped the approaching stranger said nothing,

made no requests for divine favor
to reinvite my soul that I conceive,
in a sieve universe, shaky still. Silently,
he waited till he could look directly

at me—and then he said, "Gableshu!"
I almost said, "Thank you." I knew
the routine. But then I saw into his eyes—
so I blessed him too. Why wait for a sneeze?

Ghost Busters

Once a year the crocus lifts
us up onto our wobbly ladders
to catch the specters smeared and webbed
across our boxed-in winter outlooks.

To look out past our own grimaces
the grimy ghosts gave back in frost
and howling storms across bare porches,
we climb where vision's held at bay,

bow, double hung, or custom made,
sliding, or closed in on its hinges.
Transparency is so hard to achieve—
that's why the religious use stain.

At high-tech energy efficients too,
their panes clasped on imprisoned gas,
we wield our rag and bucket traps.
No insubstantiality of view

can stop this crocus impetus to light
and clarity, so long as there's a frame,
a boxing out of world to truly see.
But live in glass houses? We can't.

We'd never survive the winter Gothic
stained by our own overblown faces.
Now these newfangled gadgets for garden hoses
don't hook the spirits like elbow grease,

the overall rubdown with warm water,
then the ammonia evenly broadcast,
muscling with cornered residues and spraying
spring's redolence, as volatile as our spirits

lifting into the ozone in the air. . .

Sustenance

At night, when slugs come out
from cracks in driveways, and push
their hungry, pasty beings
up doorway ledges, along window glass,

when cratered snails lose their way
up sterile lampposts, lit
for some other kind's vision,
feebly feelering the black universe,

this unhoused self of darkness,
that would dip like a deliberate hummingbird beak
down deep dream-sweet feed funnels,
on iridescent, metaphysically winging words,

this lame, night-debris feeder, that knows
the crawl and crush of slugs and snails
beneath larger feet in the garden,
this heart, on its own muscle, pushes out again.

One Small Kindness

Each day my neighbor
carries his dog
all the way to the park
because she's too old
to walk so far
while her son frisks along
high spirited beside them.
Motionless with arthritic ice
her little Yorkshire legs
know surrender and hope
cradled together
in his peaceful arms
that don't make the news
as he carries the blur
of hours into deep dark
with what matters.

Sheltering Cats

Hail like thorns falling everywhere from nowhere
but within a row of garbage cans—dubbed "Cat Condos"—
we laid on their sides, lined with carpet,
sweaters, and other remnants of our molting lives
that make warmth a growing need in a windy world.

Through closed lids we opened thresholds
so windows are doorways, as seeing is entrance
and a means of leaving our own little places,
so into that part of their lives clearly theirs,
we feed on such sweet furry faces!

To each a name, an eye-widening identity,
like Uncle Brownie, who nurtured his sister's litter,
and Swirl, too antsy to eat with the crowd,
Renalda and Hot Pants, a pair loyal for years,
as they're sheltering our loving alchemy.

Cat Funeral

Between the warmth of their furry circle
and the sting of another late spring,
between the cankered clouds we fly with
through the window, and the muddy leaf litter
across the patio, Dilly, grand matriarch
of generations who live in our back yard,
emerged from her black, 3-foot lean-to
with it in her mouth, a dangling smidgen
of senselessness. She dropped it at their feet,
these we call Blizzard, Snowy, and Swirl,
she'd faithfully nursed in that lean-to
all through last winter's blitzkrieg snow,
Silly-Dilly and Dilly-Dally, we'd named for her,
Chocolate, Brownie, and Stubby too, all grown
and benignly ignored by her except for
an occasional head-bumping—translation: "Hi,
how ya doin!" just passing in our garden.

And between this morning's op-ed debate
on whether Spanglish is a proper language
and Nike's women workers brutally run
to light-headed enlightenment and collapse
in Vietnam on International Women's Day,
between Aunt Helen's cold phone lines
"Don't be a wussy!" to Mike to cope
with his mother's sudden death from stroke,
I watched behind the glass, somewhere between
a distant bystander of another bruised world
and the "catwoman" the neighbors call me,
somewhere flesh and fur interface and know.
Each grown child sniffed and pawed the dead one.
Then Dilly picked it up, and they followed,
a slipshod litter procession, across
the patio, and down the garden steps,
along the lawn to the thrashing hemlocks' beds.

She clawed a hole, and they hovered round
as she buried the baby without a sound.
Who could say for sure what was going on

out there in the throes of our back yard,
but her task done, she returned to our patio,
her familial retinue following behind.
And they wrapped themselves around her,
enfolding her and licking her,
enfurring her with all they were,
upgathering her hair, her ears, her eyes,
moistening her translationless all over
in sympathy's universally mothering tongues.

Muse Relishing in the Tomato Garden

They sprawl out in sunshine
across the patio steps
like partying poolside Playboy Bunnies,

all bare ripe breasts,
playing water polo,
unabashedly sweet and firm

young flesh, meant to deliquesce
beneath the tongue of imagination.
Thin hymens, pending genitalia

licked with passion, swelling with blood.
Fleshy lascivious hearts
filled with tears when penetrated,

tears taken into one's blood.
Recumbent when fruiting like Whitman,
and ready to gender family secrets

beneath the nightshades. Coleridge would
praise the green umbilical lines
of connection, the firm grip

on the central stem, the fingerability,
the fresh and raw succulence,
the shiny sunlit self-containment.

He'd praise the non-snobbish
organic redolence of this elegance
in satin skin to other

family types like smokers and taters,
the outreaching appeal across the continents
and ages, to the Indians of Mexico,

Central America, prehistoric time,
how sliced, each disklike section
reveals the universe

of the old Indian Medicine Wheel,
like the stanza of a poem,
with living seeds symmetrically chambered

around the center as if reflected
by perceptual mirrors. He'd praise
the modern defiance of popular distinctions,

fruit or vegetable, the consummation
aimed at main course, not some
fanciness like a sugary dessert,

the pruning and processing versatility,
with conserves assuming the curves
of their containers. He'd prefer—

over the saucy young hothouse productions
openly parading their wares
for street vendors, and above

those superficially reddened
off the vine of connection
with market in mind and shipped off

unripe in flat lug boxes—
the inner sweetness of these
homegrown from seeds penned

in one's own little bed
and organically transferred
to the larger field alfresco.

So go ahead, make my day!
Did you think I'd take offense
at your sexually harassing, old slang

semblance to whatever is earthy
and whatever transmutes from the dregs
to translucent-skinned artistry,

like some beefy young woman?
Go ahead, make my day—
Call me a tomato!

A Sitting Duck's Herstory

I belong to her garden
       and to her who paints me,
layer on layer, rebrushing
       my wooden wings into feathers
every spring before her flowers.
       I am her chromatic legend,
a wee piece of her mind
       out where the neighbors walk.
My history is herstory.
       I am her solaced energy,
why they stop to look. My bounty
       is how she minds concretes—
A little wood arcs
       into her bridge. Blue gravel
seeds into her stream.
       The arms of her wind are spinning
where her flowers hone the sun,
       and sepia stones emerge as deer.
Herstory embraces history,
       how he resonates in me for her,
that nice man she bought me from,
       my cottage artisan of garden stakes,
how I knocked her off her pedals
       as she was biking by,
and he told her his life story,
       even about the prostate cancer.
I speak her aura's archeology.
       One dark night I was uprooted,
tossed in a getaway car
       with laughing fools. As I lost
all sensibility, the laugh
       was on them. They couldn't get away
with what they couldn't see.
       I had no meaning outside herstory.
Blindfolded, hanging from a tree,
       I was shot by a Polaroid,
captioned "Help me!" (lies!

they never got me to talk).
The policeman laughed at the cut-
            paste note: "IF U WAN
2 SEE YOUR DUCK ALIVE
            AGAIN SEND $1,000,000."
"Lady, please! They steal
            real statues from my garden!
Keep everything you value inside!"
            So she went home, one mote
less faith in humanity,
            and me a splinter in her heart.
But here's my favorite part,
            my mute leap into legendary—
one day she opens the boundless door
            of surprise—It's me! Brought back
from being nobody, from who knows where,
            of no use to who knows who,
a rope around my neck, scratched feet,
            a lame duck beaming herstory —
I take my rightful place in her garden.

Central Park

Labor Day

Shooting uphill, through the slow-climbing crowd,
the weight of his whole body balanced on his blade
of wheels, the skater vies for flying time
with disks, rings, boomerangs, and winged things,
footballs with fins and frisbees sent sailing
hundreds of feet at a toss, as people are filling
the skies with aerobatic stunts, and scribblers try
with paint or pen on the grass to surf on
that same airflow at the leading edge
to create their center of lift with image or language.
Into that charmed current go the speeding
bikers and skaters, helmeted like pilots,
with trailing vapors of joggers, high
on their hormones, a flock of funky crow puppets
in purple jackets and sunglasses, rocking and rapping
in sync, with hugs for the clapping, tapping kids.
New York's native kaleidoscope is climbing the notes
in caftans and jeans, saris and jumpsuits—
a ring of steel drummers is inviting guests
to sit in and take off, a guy plays light
on a homemade stringed gourd etched with a star,
a venerable jazz combo is pitching
over old songs, raising a sing-along,
as couples start rotating in tango flight
or flights of embrace out on Great Lawn,
where a lakeside crooner is grabbing the sun
on the mike as it leaps from guitar strings,
radio dials, pen clips, and flying rings,
in iridescent, overlapping scales aloft,
risen from the green grass sea of humanity
stretching summer's soaring, gliding, defying gravity
with a volleyball or kiss, a pressing lip
at a concave edge to a disk, brush, wind
instrument or word, at the megaphone of a film maker,
who looks just like Woody Allen, jump-

cutting to a horse and buggy ride,
as girls are gaining altitude through a turning rope,
each starting from a separate jumping-off place,
where fear is known to jump in the throat,
and some think of the junkies and muggers high-tailing
from dark corners for whatever they can lift,
or feel the more frightening grasp of mugger within,
and into that charmed current warmed by air
defying the hidden labor of lift from place,
NYers keep whisking me right off my page.

A Photo-Zen of Humped Shoulders

Yellowstone

From the growling land of the great caldera,
where rain and snow percolate down through cracks,
to rise again, boiling and brightly colored,
hissing and steaming in sulfurous caves,

exploding skywards in geysers' thundering,
from the land of Palpitator and Green Dragon Springs,
where rock is so hot it is pulsating,
and hot acid is a home to hardy beings,

the beauty of the civilized hunt
is still in the daring, close-up shot.
You need to see just what
you're made of by how near you can get

to wild hunger, irritation, danger, courtship
driving the shaggy-coated massiveness
with its vast bison head, as it lifts,
and you step closer to those wet nostrils

that have sniffed the fury of fireholes and fumaroles,
this humped creature that looks at you with its knowing
eye of big sky country and spacious roaming,
once killed for sport or its tongue alone.

There's a wild glory in risking goring,
or through thermal meadows, sulfuric scorching,
as you track elk scats, the ground roaring,
the males bugling, as you are picturing

that rack of antlers above your hearth,
that young one in velvet on its hummock, hanging,
that sleek leaper through lodgepoles here,
for your taking, that elegant, unperturbed head

browsing in the rain. You learn to wait
for what stills and focuses your mind, your aches

from crouching go numb, and then it raises
in full, furry, unpredictability, flash of grace,

the pure quarry shot through its inmost gusto,
in its most majestically flat-footed moment,
yours, a touch of grizzly shuffling, humped shoulder,
as you've absorbed the humps and gear on your own.

Lakeside Sinfonietta

the Adirondacks

Between the mountain-shawled lake and the seated,
shawled adults, between the shelled musicians and rows
and rows of chairs, like something out of a good dream,
          children come dancing.

Over the lakeside boulder, out onto the grass,
across the flying programs and stray committee schedules,
carrying the wind and reeds' idiom in being,
          children come dancing.

Along ardor's overflowing edge, on wet,
muddy, who-cares soles, loose in the limbs
of fluency and touching Mozart with their whole bodies,
          children come dancing.

Upgathering spin-drift and sparkle, on airs of extension,
with all the glimmer of 1000 lakes and desires
they would know in their blood, Debussy made flesh when
          children come dancing.

While one flings grass up, one marrows through
an explosion of runs, one falls into laughter and violins'
sweet staircase of strings, and all sonority is stepping when
          children come dancing.

Beyond whatever whittles through the woodwinds of human purpose,
Beyond the ruining tempo, the mortality in our stars,
with wondrously squandering energy on pivots of identity,
          children come dancing.

Funneling Sun

Sometimes I play a game
with myself that my wish
to go back in time
to this very day and this
very bounty of my life
at this very moment has been
granted from some high-walled
future I can't begin to imagine
and I am younger as I am
but hadn't seen over those high
concrete blocks in everyday living
to bask in the luminous lake
the sunshine makes as it touches
and spreads through my mind
the abundant crop of tomatoes
beefing in pots on the patio
where licking their fur to shiny
three cats leisurely curl
as Mike licks his finger and parts
sunlight in the province of his book
and bids me enter the expedition
of undaunted courage with him
on our patio with Meriwether Lewis
and ringing enters the native sunshine
signaling from those we love
calling from the interior
of their own private expeditions
maybe our son and his wife reporting
on the bid they made for a house
maybe my mom bidding me
to drive her to see dad in the home
or a friend organizing the Friday brunch
to feast together after Thanksgiving
with all our children and all their loves
and I am so glad in this wellspring
my wish has come true to my life

About the Author

Gayl Teller is the author of two volumes of poetry, **Shorehaven** and **At the Intersection of Everything You Have Ever Loved**, and the chapbook of poetry **Moving Day**. Her many accolades include the Edgar Allan Poe Prize for Literary Excellence, the Peninsula Library Poetry Prize, and poetry awards from the National Federation of State Poetry Societies, the National League of American PEN Women, and The *Connecticut Writer*.

Gayl Teller is the founder and director of the New York State Council on the Arts Poetry Reading Series at the Mid-Island Y, Plainview, NY, since 1996. She has been teaching in the English Department of Hofstra University since 1985 and has conducted numerous poetry seminars and workshops under the auspices of Poets and Writers at numerous universities and poetry centers. Her poems are widely published and anthologized, most recently in the award-winning **Bronx Accent: A Literary and Pictorial History of the Borough,** and her reviews of poetry books have appeared frequently in **Small Press Review**. She lives with her husband and cats in Long Island.

About the Artist

Diana Dopson resides in Austin, Texas. She received her M.F.A. in photography (2001) and her M.A. in art history (1997) from the University of Oregon. She completed undergraduate degrees from the University of Texas at Austin, where she was valedictorian and an All-American tennis player. She was awarded the Edilia and François-Auguste de Montêquin Fellowship by the Society of Architectural Historians in 1997 for her research on the Puebloan architecture of the American Southwest. In 1998, she completed the Corso Internazionale sull'Architettura di Andrea Palladio in Vicenza, Italy. For the past six years, she has led walking tours in Italy and Texas for Butterfield and Robinson. She is also an Austin board member of the Nature Conservancy.